THE AWESOM[E]

Hilarious & Heavenly Cartoons

JONNY HAWKINS

HARVEST HOUSE PUBLISHERS
EUGENE, OREGON

Cover by Dugan Design Group, Bloomington, Minnesota

THE AWESOME BOOK OF HILARIOUS AND HEAVENLY CARTOONS
Copyright © 2012 by Jonny Hawkins
Published by Harvest House Publishers
Eugene, Oregon 97402
www.harvesthousepublishers.com

ISBN 978-0-7369-4917-0 (pbk.)
ISBN 978-0-7369-4918-7 (eBook)

Printed in the United States of America

12 13 14 15 16 17 18 19 20 / BP-SK / 10 9 8 7 6 5 4 3 2 1

**"God wants to know what
your speaking fees are."**

*"Then the LORD's anger burned against Moses and he said,
'What about your brother, Aaron the Levite?...
He will speak to the people for you'" (Exodus 4:14,17).*

THEME: AARON

"At this point, that seems a little pie in the sky."

"Look up at the sky and count the stars—if indeed you can count them...So shall your offspring be" (Genesis 15:5).

THEME: ABRAHAMIC COVENANT

**"I'm the angel food cake angel.
I bring you peace, hope, and comfort food."**

"Are not all angels ministering spirits sent to serve those who will inherit salvation?" (Hebrews 1:14).

THEME: ANGELS

"You're missing a wing nut."

"Do not forget to show hospitality to strangers, for by so doing some people have shown hospitality to angels without knowing it" (Hebrews 13:2).

THEME: ANGELS

"You named me rabbit?
Is the plural form 'rabbi'?"

*"The LORD God had formed out of the ground all the wild
animals and all the birds in the sky. He brought them to the
man to see what he would name them; and whatever the man
called each living creature, that was its name" (Genesis 2:19).*

THEME: ANIMAL NAMES

"No—think outside the box."

"How high are you ascending?"

Genuine leather

**"We got his name from the Bible—
Jonathan David Obadiah Gideon.
For short, we're calling him J-Dog."**

"Now, quit sinning and
get these last two outs!"

"When Jesus saw the crowds, he went up on a
mountainside and sat down. His disciples came to
him, and he began to teach them" (Matthew 5:1-2).

THEME: BASEBALL

"I know there's one around here. These are bear tracts."

"And you also will bear witness" (John 15:27 ESV).

*"The word of the Lord spread widely
and grew in power" (Acts 19:20).*

Theme: Bible

"You don't double click anything, son. It's a Bible."

"Let the word of Christ dwell in you richly" (Colossians 3:16 ESV).

THEME: BIBLE

**"Can you come back in five minutes?
Right now, his eye is on the sparrow."**

---

*"Are not two sparrows sold for a penny? Yet not one of them will
fall to the ground outside your Father's care" (Matthew 10:29).*

Theme: bird-watching

"I don't reap or gather into barns, but occasionally I've gotta sew."

"Look at the birds of the air; they do not sow or reap or store away in barns, and yet your heavenly Father feeds them. Are you not much more valuable than they?" (Matthew 6:26).

THEME: BIRDS

**"Come, let us see this One...
and spread the word via satellite..."**

*"Where is the one who has been born king of
the Jews? We saw his star when it rose and have
come to worship him" (Matthew 2:2).*

THEME: BIRTH OF CHRIST

**"It's Paul and Moses...part
of my Bible-head collection."**

Growing up James

*"I saw none of the other apostles—only James,
the Lord's brother" (Galatians 1:19).*

THEME: BROTHERS

The Camel Whisperer

"The righteous care for the needs of their animals, but the kindest acts of the wicked are cruel" (Proverbs 12:10).

<small>Theme: camel</small>

Jesus—the original child advocate

"Jesus said, 'Let the little children come to me,
and do not hinder them, for the kingdom of heaven
belongs to such as these'" (Matthew 19:14).

THEME: CHILDREN

"Mom says the best Christmas deal is that *Jesus* saves."

"I am the gate; whoever enters through me will be saved" (John 10:9).

THEME: CHRISTMAS

"This is *one* gift box I won't return."

"I'm going in for a faith lift."

"Encourage one another and build each other up,
just as in fact you are doing" (1 Thessalonians 5:11).

Theme: church

"Now you are the body of Christ, and each
one of you is a part of it" (1 Corinthians 12:27).

THEME: CHURCH

"He is a God of order. The shortest verse in the Bible says it—Jesus swept."

"Jesus wept" (John 11:35).

Theme: cleanliness

**Billy Zillman gets the call
to the mission field.**

*"Go into all the world and preach the gospel
to all creation"* (Mark 16:15).

THEME: COMMISSION

"I don't know about this 'bear one another's burdens' stuff. When does the tranquilizer wear off?"

"So, how's your unconditional love life?"

"Follow God's example, therefore, as dearly loved children and walk in the way of love, just as Christ loved us and gave himself up for us as a fragrant offering and sacrifice to God" (Ephesians 5:1-2).

THEME: COMPASSION

**"It's 'In the beginning,'
Billy, not 'Back in the day.'"**

*"In the beginning God created the
heavens and the earth" (Genesis 1:1).*

THEME: CREATION

**Beware of being cross-eyed…
it just might stick.**

*"May I never boast except in the cross of
our Lord Jesus Christ"* (Galatians 6:14).

THEME: CROSS

"You make known to me the path of life; you will fill me with joy in your presence, with eternal pleasures at your right hand" (Psalm 16:11).

THEME: CROSSROADS

"When the sky went dark, the Son shined through."

"Darkness came over the whole land until three in the afternoon, for the sun stopped shining. And the curtain of the temple was torn in two. Jesus called out with a loud voice, 'Father, into your hands I commit my spirit'" (Luke 23:44-46).

THEME: CRUCIFIXION

"I pray and exercise three times a day. I think you'll find my accusers much more succulent."

"Three times a day he got down on his knees and prayed, giving thanks to his God, just as he had done before... God sent his angel, and he shut the mouths of the lions" (Daniel 6:10,22).

THEME: DANIEL

"No, but you *can* find a date with destiny and love eternal in *this* little black book."

"Dear friends, let us love one another, for love comes from God. Everyone who loves has been born of God and knows God" (1 John 4:7).

THEME: DATING

Moments before David the shepherd boy slays the lion

"When a lion or a bear came and carried off a sheep from the flock, I went after it, struck it and rescued the sheep from its mouth. When it turned on me, I seized it by its hair, struck it and killed it" (1 Samuel 17:34-35).

Theme: David

The origin of deviled ham

"The demons begged Jesus, 'Send us among the pigs; allow us to go into them.' He gave them permission, and the impure spirits came out and went into the pigs. The herd, about two thousand in number, rushed down the steep bank into the lake and were drowned" (Mark 5:12-13).

THEME: DEMONS

"I'm busy with the net right now... can I follow you on Twitter?"

"'Come, follow me,' Jesus said, 'and I will send you out to fish for people.' At once they left their nets and followed him" (Matthew 4:19-20).

THEME: DISCIPLES

"Watch your life and doctrine closely" (1 Timothy 4:16).

Theme: dogma

"What? No childlike faith?"

"Truly I tell you, anyone who will not receive the kingdom of God like a little child will never enter it" (Luke 18:17).

THEME: DOUBT

"It was called the Last Supper because after that, they invented potlucks."

"He will show you a large upper room furnished and ready; there prepare for us" (Mark 14:15 ESV).

THEME: EATING

"When you fast, put oil on your head and wash your face,
so that it will not be obvious to others that you are fasting,
but only to your Father, who is unseen; and your Father,
who sees what is done in secret, will reward you" (Matthew 6:17-18).

THEME: EATING

"No, it has nothing to do with global warming."

"The fire of the LORD fell and burned up the sacrifice, the wood, the stones and the soil, and also licked up the water in the trench. When all the people saw this, they fell prostrate and cried, 'The LORD—he is God! The LORD—he is God!'" (1 Kings 18:38-39)

THEME: ELIJAH

**"How's that for blazing horsepower?
Now, watch when I shift into second."**

*"Suddenly a chariot of fire and horses of fire appeared
and separated the two of them, and Elijah went
up to heaven in a whirlwind" (2 Kings 2:11).*

THEME: ELIJAH

"They must have had some form of e-mail.
The apostle Paul wrote the *e*pistles."

*"Paul, a servant of Christ Jesus...to all in Rome who are
loved by God and called to be his holy people" (Romans 1:1,7).*

THEME: E-MAIL

One of the few Pauline epistles not canonized

*"Let the king and Haman come tomorrow to
the banquet I will prepare for them" (Esther 5:8).*

Theme: Esther

Gallows humor

"The king...gave orders in writing that...[Haman] and his sons should be hanged on the gallows" (Esther 9:25 ESV).

Theme: Esther

"An apple, eh? Where are the nutrition facts?"

"When the woman saw that the fruit of the tree was good for food and pleasing to the eye, and also desirable for gaining wisdom, she took some and ate it" (Genesis 3:6).

THEME: EVE

**City Church believed in
applying a little pressure.**

---

*"A wife of noble character who can find?
She is worth far more than rubies" (Proverbs 31:10).*

THEME: EXPECTATIONS

Faith cometh by hearing

"Faith comes from hearing the message, and the message is heard through the word about Christ" (Romans 10:17).

THEME: FAITH

"I would have gone to the upper room also, but I'm afraid of heights."

"God has not given us a spirit of fear, but of power and of love and of a sound mind" (2 Timothy 1:7 NKJV).

THEME: FEAR

"At first I thought there were lions among us, but then I realized it was 5000 growling stomachs."

"The number of those who ate was about five thousand men, besides women and children" (Matthew 14:21).

THEME: FEEDING OF 5000

"There will be coffee and donuts after Sunday school, and don't forget potluck after the service. This evening's sermon is titled 'Our Body Is a Temple,' followed by pie and ice cream in the fellowship hall."

"Do you not know that your bodies are temples of the Holy Spirit?...
Therefore honor God with your bodies" (1 Corinthians 6:19-20).

THEME: FELLOWSHIP

"Don't you worry about burnout?"

"If we are thrown into the blazing furnace, the God we serve is able to deliver us from it" (Daniel 3:17).

THEME: FIERY FURNACE

*"Whoever can be trusted with very little can
also be trusted with much" (Luke 16:10).*

THEME: FINANCES

"Then the LORD rained brimstone and fire
on Sodom and Gomorrah, from the LORD out
of the heavens" (Genesis 19:24 NKJV).

THEME: FIRE AND BRIMSTONE

"Do you know where you'd go if you died today?"

"Quite the opposite.
I have it made in the shade."

"He must become greater; I must become less" (John 3:30).

THEME: FOLLOWING CHRIST

"Well done, good and faithful servant."

"Well done, good and faithful servant! You have been faithful with a few things; I will put you in charge of many things. Come and share your master's happiness!" (Matthew 25:21).

THEME: FOOD

"John's clothes were made of camel's hair,
and he had a leather belt around his waist.
His food was locusts and wild honey" (Matthew 3:4).

THEME: FOOD

Jumbo could forgive the poacher's indiscretion, but it would take some dulling of the gray matter to forget.

"Be kind and compassionate to one another, forgiving each other, just as in Christ God forgave you" (Ephesians 4:32).

THEME: FORGIVENESS

"Choose for yourselves this day whom you will serve…But as for me and my household, we will serve the LORD" (Joshua 24:15).

THEME: FREE WILL

"No, you are my second best. God is my BFF."

"I have called you friends, for everything that I learned from my Father I have made known to you" (John 15:15).

Theme: friends

"Toadally."

*"Trust in the LORD forever, for the LORD,
the LORD himself, is the Rock eternal"* (Isaiah 26:4).

THEME: FROG

"Frog leg soup! Now I'm hopping mad!"

*"Aaron stretched out his hand over the waters of Egypt,
and the frogs came up and covered the land" (Exodus 8:6).*

THEME: FROGS

**It's hard to bear fruit
when you're a couch potato.**

"And this is my dad. He begot me."

"Abraham begot Isaac, Isaac begot Jacob, and Jacob begot Judah and his brothers" (Matthew 1:2 NKJV).

THEME: GENEALOGY

"I'm giving a 10-spot to these visiting missionaries. I have no idea what Lefty's doing."

"When you give to the needy, do not let your left hand know what your right hand is doing" (Matthew 6:3).

THEME: GIVING

"Saul, I mean Paul, you've really got to stop kicking against the goads."

"Saul, Saul, why do you persecute me? It is hard for you to kick against the goads" (Acts 26:14).

THEME: GOADS

"I'd be very grateful for *anyone's* kidney, but I'm a man after God's own heart."

"I have found David son of Jesse, a man after my own heart; he will do everything I want him to do" (Acts 13:22).

THEME: GOD'S HEART

"God so loved the world that he gave his one and only Son, that whoever believes in him shall not perish but have eternal life" (John 3:16).

THEME: GOD'S LOVE

"Something about an overactive thyroid."

"A champion named Goliath, who was from Gath, came out of the Philistine camp. His height was six cubits and a span" (1 Samuel 17:4).

THEME: GOLIATH

**"Cut off his head? What if
I just give him a stern noogie?"**

---

*"David ran and stood over him. He took hold of the Philistine's
sword and drew it from the sheath. After he killed him,
he cut off his head with the sword" (1 Samuel 17:51).*

THEME: GOLIATH

**Jesus seeks and finds his lost sheep
without a search engine or GPS.**

*"I am the good shepherd; I know my sheep and my sheep
know me—just as the Father knows me and I know the
Father—and I lay down my life for the sheep" (John 10:14-15).*

Theme: good shepherd

"I've met Pretty Nice Polly and Friendly Fran...but who is this Amazing Grace I keep hearing about?"

"It is by grace you have been saved" (Ephesians 2:5).

THEME: GRACE

"Tell me about this 30-day grace period."

"I knew it! I knew it was you who wrote that prophetic book! I could tell by your haggy eye!"

"The word of the LORD came through the prophet Haggai" (Haggai 1:1).

THEME: HAGGAI

"God knows the very number
of hares on his head."

*"And even the very hairs of your head
are all numbered"* (Matthew 10:30).

THEME: HAIRS

"I'm reading Hebrews 11—the Hall of Faith. Do you suspect any of them used performance enhancers?"

"Now faith is confidence in what we hope for and assurance about what we do not see. This is what the ancients were commended for" (Hebrews 11:1-2).

THEME: HALL OF FAITH

PowerPoint in the Bible

"Suddenly the fingers of a human hand appeared
and wrote on the plaster of the wall, near the
lampstand in the royal palace" (Daniel 5:5).

THEME: HANDWRITING ON THE WALL

Hydrotherapy in Bible times

*"There is in Jerusalem near the Sheep Gate a pool,
which in Aramaic is called Bethesda...Here a
great number of disabled people used to lie—the
blind, the lame, the paralyzed" (John 5:2-3).*

THEME: HEALING

"I loved your sermon, but you didn't answer one critical question: Is there big hair in heaven?"

"We have heard of your faith in Christ Jesus and of the love you have for all God's people—the faith and love that spring from the hope stored up for you in heaven" (Colossians 1:4-5).

THEME: HEAVEN

"How awesome is this place! This is none other than the house of God; this is the gate of heaven" (Genesis 28:17).

THEME: HEAVEN

**"And see us again on
Thursday for karaoke night."**

*"Suddenly a great company of the heavenly host appeared
with the angel, praising God and saying, 'Glory
to God in the highest heaven, and on earth peace to
those on whom his favor rests'" (Luke 2:13-14).*

THEME: HEAVENLY HOST

**"You can find your sister later.
Seek ye first the kingdom of God."**

*"Seek first his kingdom and his righteousness, and all
these things will be given to you as well" (Matthew 6:33).*

THEME: HIDE AND SEEK

**"You had how many in the net?
Peter, are you telling another fish story?"**

**"I just got a log removed.
Hey, do I see a speck?"**

*"You hypocrite, first take the log out of your own
eye, and then you will see clearly to take the speck
out of your brother's eye" (Matthew 7:5 ESV).*

THEME: HYPOCRISY

"I could really go for some heavenly hash."

*"Taste and see that the LORD is good; blessed is
the one who takes refuge in him" (Psalm 34:8).*

"How about *single*-minded?"

"The one who doubts is like a wave of the sea, blown and tossed by the wind...Such a person is double-minded and unstable in all they do" (James 1:6,8).

THEME: ICE CREAM

"I was jailed for carving the wrong idol and now I have to make Baal."

"All the people went to the temple of Baal and tore it down.
They smashed the altars and idols" (2 Chronicles 23:17).

THEME: IDOL WORSHIP

"Can you teach me some angel-wrestling moves?"

"Jacob was left alone, and a man wrestled with him till daybreak... Then the man said, 'Your name will no longer be Jacob, but Israel, because you have struggled with God and with humans and have overcome'" (Genesis 32:24,28).

THEME: JACOB

"Oh, you mean Jezebel?"

"[Ahab] married Jezebel daughter of Ethbaal
king of the Sidonians, and began to serve Baal
and worship him" (1 Kings 16:31).

THEME: JEZEBEL

"Pretty much everything."

"Could you put my honey locust on the warmer? I'm hip-deep in baptisms today."

"John's clothes were made of camel's hair, and he had a leather belt around his waist. His food was locusts and wild honey. People went out to him from Jerusalem and all Judea and the whole region of the Jordan. Confessing their sins, they were baptized by him in the Jordan River" (Matthew 3:4-6).

THEME: JOHN THE BAPTIST

**The great fish found all of
this very hard to swallow.**

"The LORD provided a huge fish to swallow Jonah" (Jonah 1:17).

THEME: JONAH

**After his whale of a time,
Jonah wears his throwback outfit.**

*"The LORD commanded the fish,
and it vomited Jonah onto dry land" (Jonah 2:10).*

THEME: JONAH

Joseph and the hoodie of many colors

"Israel loved Joseph more than any other of his sons, because he was the son of his old age. And he made him a robe of many colors" (Genesis 37:3 ESV).

THEME: JOSEPH

**"I ate fast food, and now
I have a coat of many colors."**

*"Israel loved Joseph more than any other of his sons,
because he was the son of his old age. And he made
him a robe of many colors" (Genesis 37:3 ESV).*

THEME: JOSEPH

"God says no vuvuzelas."

"At the sound of the trumpet, when the men gave a loud shout, the wall collapsed; so everyone charged straight in, and they took the city" (Joshua 6:20).

THEME: JOSHUA

"Wow—king at age eight! I made the fifth level on Kingdom Warriors on my Zbox…that's kinda the same thing."

"Josiah was eight years old when he became king, and he reigned in Jerusalem thirty-one years" (2 Kings 22:1).

THEME: JOSIAH

"Today we learned how to pronounce judgment."

"Do not judge, or you too will be judged. For in the same way you judge others, you will be judged, and with the measure you use, it will be measured to you" (Matthew 7:1-2).

THEME: JUDGMENT

"Make up your mind and stick
with it. Let your 'yay!' be 'yay!'
and your 'neigh' be 'neigh.'"

*"Let your yea be yea; and your nay, nay;
lest ye fall into condemnation" (James 5:12 KJV).*

THEME: KEEPING YOUR WORD

**"Why did Adam and Eve have kids?
So they could be weedin' the
Garden of Eden."**

*"Cursed is the ground because of you...It will produce
thorns and thistles for you" (Genesis 3:17-18).*

THEME: KIDS

"Assuredly, I say to you, till heaven and earth pass away, one jot or one tittle will by no means pass from the law till all is fulfilled" (Matthew 5:18 NKJV).

THEME: LAW

Lazarus was the life of the party.

*"Jesus said to them, 'Take off the grave
clothes and let him go'" (John 11:44).*

Theme: Lazarus

"I guess He's trying to teach me something about being longsuffering."

"Put on therefore, as the elect of God, holy and beloved, bowels of mercies, kindness, humbleness of mind, meekness, longsuffering..." (Colossians 3:12 KJV).

THEME: LONGSUFFERING

"She always wanted to be a pillar in her community and the salt of the earth."

"Lot's wife looked back, and she became a pillar of salt" (Genesis 19:26).

THEME: LOT'S WIFE

"My love for you is more
a guppy love than agape."

"Love your neighbor as yourself" (Mark 12:31).

**"No, it's not dandruff, Moses.
You have a bad case of manna."**

"The Holy Spirit will come on you, and the power of
the Most High will overshadow you. So the holy one to
be born will be called the Son of God" (Luke 1:35).

THEME: MARY

"Well done."

"Anyone who lives on milk, being still an infant, is not acquainted with the teaching about righteousness. But solid food is for the mature" (Hebrews 5:13-14).

THEME: MEAT

**"Don't let it bother you—
Methuselah calls *everybody* 'kiddo.'"**

Rock of Ages

*"Methuselah lived a total of 969 years,
and then he died" (Genesis 5:27).*

THEME: METHUSELAH

"Consistent breathing."

"Methuselah lived a total of 969 years, and then he died" (Genesis 5:27).

Theme: Methuselah

Methuselah and his offspring

*"Methuselah lived a total of 969 years,
and then he died" (Genesis 5:27).*

THEME: METHUSELAH

"And if anyone is lactose intolerant, over there we have the land of silk and honey."

"I have come down to rescue them from the hand of the Egyptians and to bring them up out of that land into a good and spacious land, a land flowing with milk and honey" (Exodus 3:8).

THEME: MILK AND HONEY

The origin of the No Bridge Club

"Peter got down out of the boat, walked on the water and came toward Jesus" (Matthew 14:29).

THEME: MIRACLES

"Let's play...but remember, no man can serve two masters."

Adventures at Horeb

"The LORD answered Moses... 'Strike the rock, and water will come out of it for the people to drink'" (Exodus 17:5-6).

THEME: MOSES

"We can help. We're carpenter ants."

"Hey, could we have some volunteers to stay and help clean up?"

"I don't know about you, but I'm getting kind of tired of these fire drills."

"I can't believe my head was in the sand and I missed the boat. (Sniff, sniff...) I feel so ostracized!"

"Pairs of clean and unclean animals...came to Noah and entered the ark, as God had commanded Noah. And after the seven days the floodwaters came on the earth" (Genesis 7:8-10).

THEME: NOAH

**"Jesus appreciated the widow's mite...
now I'd like to give my two cents' worth."**

*"Calling his disciples to him, Jesus said,
'Truly I tell you, this poor widow has put more into
the treasury than all the others'" (Mark 12:43).*

THEME: OFFERING

"Sorry, Malchus, for cutting off your ear. In truth, I was trying to get a head."

"Simon Peter, who had a sword, drew it and struck the high priest's servant, cutting off his right ear. (The servant's name was Malchus)" (John 18:10).

THEME: PETER

**When the rooster crowed,
Peter had his wake-up call.**

---

*"Before the rooster crows, you will
disown me three times"* (Matthew 26:75).

THEME: PETER

"We're Israelites…can we *have* pigtails?"

"The pig…is unclean for you" (Leviticus 11:7).

THEME: PIGTAILS

"If the people won't cry out with praise to God, we will. We're a Christian rock band."

"I tell you... if they keep quiet,
the stones will cry out" (Luke 19:40).

THEME: PRAISE

"But when you pray, go into your room, close the door and pray to your Father, who is unseen. Then your Father, who sees what is done in secret, will reward you" (Matthew 6:6).

THEME: PRAYER

"Looks like we've got ourselves a pen pal."

"He went and hired himself out to a citizen of that country, who sent him to his fields to feed pigs. He longed to fill his stomach with the pods that the pigs were eating, but no one gave him anything" (Luke 15:15-16).

THEME: PRODIGAL SON

"It's an advocacy group for leftovers."

"I've spent all day turning from sin.
Whew, now I've got vertigo."

"They broke bread in their homes and ate together with glad and sincere hearts" (Acts 2:46).

THEME: RESTAURANTS

"There was a violent earthquake, for an angel of the Lord came down from heaven and, going to the tomb, rolled back the stone and sat on it" (Matthew 28:2).

THEME: RESURRECTION

"Samson killed a lion with his bare hands? He must have taken hapkido."

"The Spirit of the LORD came powerfully upon him so that he tore the lion apart with his bare hands" (Judges 14:6).

THEME: SAMSON

Getting elected to the
Sanhedrin student council

"Woe to you, teachers of the law and Pharisees,
you hypocrites... On the outside you appear to
people as righteous but on the inside you are full of
hypocrisy and wickedness" (Matthew 23:27-28).

THEME: SANHEDRIN

"The Bible says, 'All have sinned and fall short…' I can relate to that."

"All have sinned and fall short of the glory of God" (Romans 3:23).

THEME: SIN

"If you do not do what is right, sin is crouching at your door; it desires to have you, but you must rule over it" (Genesis 4:7).

Theme: sin

**"Yes, I'm sure of it, officer.
This is where my old sin nature died."**

*"We know that our old self was crucified with him
so that the body ruled by sin might be done away with,
that we should no longer be slaves to sin" (Romans 6:6).*

THEME: SIN NATURE

"I'm needing to get to Oklahoma. Can you lead me beside Stillwater?"

"He makes me lie down in green pastures. He leads me beside still waters (Psalm 23:2 ESV).

THEME: STILL WATERS

"For the last time, there *is no* section with Sudoku!"

"You study the Scriptures diligently" (John 5:39).

THEME: SUDOKU

"I tried to decide where to deposit my amount: in a rich soil bank or a savings and loam."

"He who had received the one talent went and dug in the ground and hid his master's money" (Matthew 25:18 ESV).

THEME: TALENTS

**"You do Bible studies in your home, eh?
Tell me about these minor prophets."**

---

*"If you owe taxes, pay taxes; if revenue, then revenue;
if respect, then respect; if honor, then honor" (Romans 13:7).*

THEME: TAXES

"When the LORD finished speaking to Moses on Mount Sinai, he gave him the two tablets of the covenant law, the tablets of stone inscribed by the finger of God" (Exodus 31:18).

THEME: TEN COMMANDMENTS

"After your sermon on tithing, I want to give 110 percent!"

**A gentle tongue is a tree of life.
A mean one…is just bark.**

*"A gentle tongue is a tree of life, but perverseness
in it breaks the spirit" (Proverbs 15:4 ESV).*

THEME: TONGUE

Jesus does the ultimate recycling.

"If anyone is in Christ, he is a new creation. The old has passed away; behold, the new has come" (2 Corinthians 5:17 ESV).

THEME: TRANSFORMATION

"You want a worldwide cruise for 40 days and 40 nights? I may Noah guy."

"You are to bring into the ark two of all living creatures, male and female, to keep them alive with you" (Genesis 6:19-20).

THEME: TRAVEL

"So, you're saying we're unequally yolked?"

"Do not be yoked together with unbelievers" (2 Corinthians 6:14).

THEME: UNEQUALLY YOKED

"Honey, I've got something for you to stand on that's a little less helter-skelter."

"Therefore everyone who hears these words of mine and puts them into practice is like a wise man who built his house on the rock" (Matthew 7:24).

THEME: WALL STREET

"According to TruthQuest, the way to
get to heaven is to get off the Highway to
Hell, take the Narrow Way, and follow the
Romans Road that leads to the cross walk."

*"I am the way and the truth and the life. No one comes
to the Father except through me" (John 14:6).*

THEME: WAY TO HEAVEN

"Hold it! That thing is sharper than a two-edged sword!"

"The word of God is alive and active. Sharper than any double-edged sword, it penetrates even to dividing soul and spirit, joints and marrow; it judges the thoughts and attitudes of the heart" (Hebrews 4:12).

THEME: WEAPON

"Then the LORD said to Moses, 'I will rain down bread from heaven for you'" (Exodus 16:4).

THEME: WILDERNESS

"The LORD's anger burned against Israel and he made them wander in the wilderness forty years, until the whole generation of those who had done evil in his sight was gone" (Numbers 32:13).

THEME: WILDERNESS

Cana wine tasting

"The master of the banquet tasted the water that had been turned into wine…He called the bridegroom aside and said… 'You have saved the best till now'" (John 2:9-10).

THEME: WINE

"I was trying to explain why she was the weaker vessel, and she put me in a headlock and punched me out."

"Husbands, in the same way be considerate as you live with your wives, and treat them with respect as the weaker partner and as heirs with you of the gracious gift of life, so that nothing will hinder your prayers" (1 Peter 3:7).

THEME: WOMEN

Scripture Index

Topical Index